Live the Life of Your Dreams: 33 Tips for Inspired Living

With grace

By Laura Ponticello

DIVINE PHOENIX

Published by Divine Phoenix
Divine Phoenix Books may be ordered by
www.divinephoenixbooks.com

Graphic Design: Chris Moebs

Certain stock imagery © Shutterstock.
Author Photo ©Laure Lillie Photography

ISBN-13: 978-0-9853915-5-3
ISBN-10: 0985391553

First Edition, April 2014
Printed in the United States of America
Divine Phoenix Date: 4/15/14

Praise for **Live the Life of Your Dreams: 33 Tips for Inspired Living**

"*Live the Life of Your Dreams* is a thought provoking look at simple measures to improve your life. It provides many suggestions for changing your life for the better, and while the book is written with women in mind, it bridges the gender gap and applies equally to men.
– Ed Little, CEO Delta Marketing Dynamics

"As a student of self-help books, I'm always looking for authentic inspirational reads. Laura offers heartfelt advice based on her own experiences as well as her findings from having surveyed women from all over the country-women, I'm sure, like you and me."
- Christine A. Krahling, Editor, blogger and book club facilitator

"I just read the sample chapter- it was amazing and inspiring! It is true we do need to take the time for ourselves as my mom always said, 'Stop and smell the roses!'" – Judith Touey, Pennsylvania

"Laura Ponticello is a gift to the New Earth. She not only inspires, she IS inspired. It's no accident that her new and prescient book, 33 is the sacred heart, ascension, light and love. This book is Laura's gift to us, written in light with love for those seeking to live an inspired, sacred, full life."
– Melina C, Woman Entrepreneur

"I'm looking forward to the publication of your book! The book really resonates with what I have read so far!" – Paula Bob, Blossoming Possibilities

"Laura Ponticello was a constant source of inspiration for me when I needed it most. She showed loving support and guidance while I was writing my book and I really feel that God brought her into my life to help me through that time. She believed in me even when I didn't and I thank God for her presence in my life; she is truly a bright source of Light." - Elizabeth Wright, Author of "*I & Eye, A Guide to Vibrational Healing and My Transformational Journey to the Light*"

"Laura is a woman of wisdom, insight and authenticity. Her written words weave a storyline that can be found in most of our personal lives, sharing the tips that give these experiences an inspired perspective to turn an ordinary life into an extraordinary life. Thank you, Laura for your deeply expressed wisdom in your writing"
– Lorraine White, entrepreneur and mother

"Your words are truly inspiring. I am grateful that there are women like you who write inspirational books and give talks to those of us who are open to listen and to learn from you. I will be buying your book and perhaps a few more for friends who share my journey. "
– Nettie, New York

"Laura Ponticello has written a book I want to keep near my side always. She has traveled a long and arduous path in life and learned many lessons, which inspire me and remind me to tend my own garden and not focus on what other gardeners are planting. I recommend Laura's book to people who want to transition to the next level and manifest their dreams with ease and joy." - Judith Fine-Sarchielli, Marketing Coach and Author, *Cookbook/Memoirs of A Gluten-Free Gypsy*

"*Live the Life of Your Dreams : 33 Tips for Inspired Living* reminds women of our common connections: we are the same and if we would pull together as one, our spirit and love can repair and reunite the entire world, bringing it back to a love-filled civilization rather than the hatred-filled place it has become. I'll keep this wonderful book on my nightstand!"
- Denise A. Schoeneck, New York

"Laura's book is a refreshingly positive work of art that makes you take a long hard look at how you live your life. Her words of wisdom, and the tips she shares in this book, will inspire you to take great care of your heart and live life to the fullest everyday! There is no doubt in my mind that Laura's book will have a significant impact on women around the world, influencing them to take charge of their lives, improve their overall health and well-being and dream." – Lisa Jo Greenfield, Mom and Entrepreneur

Dedication

To my mother, Beverly and my grandmother, Nana Rose for standing tall in the face of adversity and instilling faith in me.

Acknowledgements

First and foremost, I give praise to my angels, guides and God for inspiring my journey. I also give thanks to my family for supporting me.

I honor the women who shared their personal stories and inspired me to write this book; your wisdom illuminated my personal path.

Thank you to my friend and mentor, Dr. Jill Little, and Ed Little, who provided valuable insight in the early stages of this book. Thanks also to Sheila Applegate for her guidance beyond this dimension and the gift of my spiritual pen.

With gratitude to Karen Wallingford, who helped edit this work and provided creative input, and Christine Krahling whose editorial expertise made the final version of this book – a better read. And to Chris Moebs for graphics design and support.

Contents

A Note to Readers

Dear Friends,

You know that lingering feeling that beckons you to take care of yourself? During some moments, it is stronger than others. Many times the inspiration is missing, the self-empowerment is lacking, and the general prioritization of self-care has been trumped by a myriad of other daily responsibilities.

The intention of this book is to place power in your hands and to act as an instrument of inspiration and hope. *Live the Life of Your Dreams: 33 Tips to Inspire Your Life*, is a book that can be carried anywhere- placed in your purse or on your nightstand, ready to provide a nudge of inspiration whenever you need it. Indeed, a guide to help you channel positivity and integrate healthy living tips at a moment's notice.

To best interact with this book and benefit from its message, you may want to read a page or a section and place the book down for a bit. Your reactions to a passage will guide the speed with which you absorb the content. The book can and should be used as a reference guide for inspiration.

I have surveyed women from different walks of life to uncover what inspires them in their daily lives; knowing that knowledge has the power to blossom, transform and grow. I found that women are most inspired when they are empowered and as a result, I started to teach women how to harness their personal power and create the destiny they have dreamed of in their own lives.

With my personal mantra, "**Fear can't hold you back in life,**" I share success secrets in *Live the Life of Your Dreams: 33 Tips to Inspire Your Life*. This book is a collection of healing graces, healthy practices, and inspirational words to help each of us achieve our amazing potential.

Many Blessings,
Laura Ponticello

"Just when the caterpillar thought the world was over, it became a butterfly." – English proverb.

The Symbolism of the Butterfly

As you scroll through the pages of this book, you will find butterfly imagery. I found the butterfly to be a universal symbol of transformation, change and growth. As I learned through my travels across the globe, while all women are different, they have more in common than they think. We are constantly evolving.

As I look back at my own personal experiences, I recognize that cycles of growth entailed rebirth. The cocoon state provided me nourishment to gain new insight about myself. Typically the cocoon state entails being still long enough to hear our inner voice, to slow down and be present in a day unfolding and to gain personal awareness. Cyclical times in life open us up to greater growth.

Many times, I simply couldn't see that all experiences were necessary for my evolution. Think of moments in time when we lose a loved one, take on a new job, become an empty nester as our child goes off to college – we are forced to sit in a space with our emotional response and how we process that response dictates our growth.

You are responsible for your journey in life. Look past the cocoon periods to know all growth is a journey but within the journey is a butterfly transforming itself. My intention in using the butterfly imagery is to remind you that when you encounter transformation, you change and evolve with each new experience, and within each moment. Also, remember you can showcase your beautiful butterfly wings.

Chapter 1

Think Big, Dream Big
Butterfly Transformation

"I will grow. I will become something new and grand, but no grander than I now am. Just as the sky will be different in a few hours, its present perfection and completeness is not deficient, so am I presently perfect and not deficient because I will be different tomorrow."- Wayne Dyer, international bestselling author

"We all have the extraordinary coded inside of us, waiting to be released." – Jean Houston, American author

My surname, Ponticello means "Little Bridge" in Italian. I was born into a religious family. We had rosary beads and religious statues on dressers and nightstands. We held mindful prayer sessions and engaged in various Catholic rites of passage- Baptism, First Penance, First Holy Communion Confirmation, and Marriage. I attended a Jesuit college where priests taught me to serve others; that which we give out to the universe is returned.

As a career woman and high achiever, I was determined to make a difference in the world. I had accomplished many things in life: I was married, living in a house with a white picket fence and had reached a level of success. I earned a six figure salary and had set up a 401k plan and saved money regularly.

I was a "Type A" individual who thrived on work. My days off were filled with grocery shopping, cooking, chores and social commitments. The thought of self-care seemed like a great concept, however not at the top of my list.

When my first marriage ended, I knew the road to the "other side" would not be easy. Guilt had kept me in a marriage that began when I was only in my twenties. As I peeled back the layers of my own heart, I had to get real with myself. My journey began to teach me to stand on my own.

Ten household items arrived from my previous house to my current living place, carelessly thrown into a cardboard box. I felt the sting of personal loss. The desire to move forward and achieve a healthy lifestyle wrestled inside me and I began to journal everything my heart had concealed for so long.

I wrote down one thing each day that gave me happiness and for which I was grateful. I surrounded myself with living things such as blooming indoor plants and a dog, because they were symbols of creation.

The profound day of transformation arrived and it was a life changing moment. Gray clouds covered the sky and the lake was a muddy blue-green with a certain magical mist hanging in the air. Rain started to pelt down.

Planting New Blossoms

I was in my vegetable garden when a feeling of conviction came over me. I kept all my legal divorce documents in a box. The flower on the front of the box reminded me of my ability to blossom again and overcome this difficult time. I placed the box with my legal documents next to my garden, and buried the documents in Mother Earth.

Then, I sprinkled a packet of zinnia seeds over the dirt and the documents. In that moment, I asked God to help me create a beautiful garden from where happiness could manifest itself in my life. Days later, I stood inside a tall field of zinnias and after that experience, everything changed. I was empowered.

Inspired Ideas for Daily Life

1. Bloom Where You Are Planted.

Sprinkle some form of zinnia seeds in your own life. Grow and blossom. As a young girl, my grandmother Nana Rose said to me: "Without rain, the flowers can't grow." Every experience serves as a foundation for you to grow and blossom.

Women Share Words of Wisdom

Over the course of the next seven years, I remarried and traveled the world, where my life experiences broadened my understanding of various cultures and religions. As I traveled to these foreign places, I realized that women have more in common than their differences. Most importantly, I encountered women who inspired me with their own wisdom.

My travels took me to Mumbai, India, San Miguel and Mexico City, to Jaffa and Jerusalem in Israel, Lake Tahoe, and recently, the Berkshires. Every trip was a conduit for my personal growth and transformation.

As I stood, hand in hand with a Christian, a Muslim, and a Hindu woman at the largest Pagoda in East Asia, I recognized that as women, we communicate in a common language, even though we speak in different dialects. As mothers, we want the best for our children. As women entrepreneurs, we desire to create something to help support ourselves.

One woman I met supported her entire family after her father died. At age fourteen, she was able to do this by creating artisan crafts.

As women constantly in flux, we crave and need the time to ourselves-quiet moments where we can catch our breath. At times, we are all things to all people at once, and neglect ourselves. This experience of coming together with women from diverse cultures showed me that the concept of self-care is important, that empowerment has the potential to bridge cultural gaps and unite- not divide-us.

I began speaking to groups of women first in small, and then larger, forums, about what inspired them in their daily lives. I told my story of sprinkling the zinnia seeds over my legal documents and how in that moment I let go of my limited beliefs. I showed photographs of me at the Wishing Bridge in Jaffa, Israel holding my zodiac sign of Aquarius, as I implored God to use me as an instrument for healing others.

Women shared with me that inspired living includes quiet practices such as meditation, yoga, journaling, breathing movements, and prayers. Physical exercise and movement in motion help women in business feel grounded in the day. Rituals and gathering circles provide forums for self-expression. Art and creative activities cultivate an expansion of self.

Empowered living means taking time for self care; the healthier we are as women, the more capable we are of supporting others. As women we must nourish our mind, body and spirit to achieve balance and healthy living.

Still Practices Inspire Wisdom

Through my own experience, I found that when I am quiet, inner wisdom pours forth. During meditation, I gain clarity. Connection with my breath for the duration of yoga invigorates me. Healthy eating makes me feel alive. Positive affirmations reemphasize that I am worthy of love.

Walks in nature or gardening outside serve as an instrument for harmony and peace for me. Gratitude is attitude, I tell myself. Soon, the steps of my day become a practice of purposeful living and being present in the moment.

The still practices bring joy and help me to unearth my inner voice. As the days pass, I shed the limited beliefs of "I cannot," and change my inner dialogue to: "I can if it's in alignment with my true self." Life becomes a series of walking miracles unfolding in front of my eyes.

My power to manifest my future began when I realized that I blossomed in new situations. I gave myself permission to dream big dreams. I came to understand that, like Buddha once said: *"What we think, we become. What we believe about ourselves can become our reality. "*

Inspired Ideas for Daily Life

2. Concentrate on Your Breath.

Inhale to the count of three. Place your hand on your abdomen, and exhale. Repeat, inhale to three, and exhale to count of three. Do this for five minutes. As you breathe in, say to yourself, "I welcome joy." As you breathe out, tell yourself, "I release fear and stress."

3. Seek refuge in nature.

My dog, Bunny, is a bundle of energy. She is a great reason for me to experience new terrain, parks, trails and the landscape of my own green grass. As I walk Bunny, I notice that nature has a subtle energy that seems to invigorate me. With each step I take with Bunny, I say out loud, "I give gratitude for today."

The Butterfly Breaks Free

"Happiness is like the butterfly: the more you chase it, the more it will elude you. But if you turn your attention to other things. It will come and sit softly on your shoulder."
– Henry David Thoreau, American poet.

A caterpillar has a gestation period where it moves from a cocoon state to eventually becoming a butterfly. This period of metamorphosis can easily be compared to our own personal growth–it is gradual, and each stage provides nourishment.

Shedding our shell and rebuilding ourselves takes time.

Caterpillars spin thread from their mouths which they use to bind together for shelter. During this time, the caterpillar changes into a butterfly. When we turn inward to nourish ourselves, we are allowing our own cocoon to build the capacity to find inner strength. It is then we can sense and feel our wings, our beauty, and our inner power.

Our transformation can be compared to the butterfly. As we spread our wings, we find new experiences expand our growth, and enhance our journey along the path of life. We constantly evolve, blossom and grow.

Reflections for the Reader

A place for you to pen your thoughts and ideas or pause enough to notice your magnificence.

Food for Thought......

♥The analogy of the butterfly is presented in this chapter, as an example of transformation. At what times in your life, have you been like the butterfly and how do you continue to grow and transform into the fullness of who you are?

Chapter 2
Fear Can't Hold You Back
Passionately with Purpose

"Nothing in life is to be feared. It is only to be understood." – Marie Curie, physicist and chemist

"You will either step forward into growth or you will step back in safety." – Abraham Maslow, physiologist best known for creating Maslow's Hierarchy of Needs

I vividly recall the day I met Jennifer Tom. Jennifer's hazel eyes and auburn hair struck a chord with me, as in her reflection, I saw a younger image of my grandmother, Nana Rose. Nana and Jennifer were both diagnosed with breast cancer in their thirties.

Nana was a first grade teacher, and would take calls from newly-diagnosed women who were contemplating radiation. Her faith-filled views helped her overstep fear, and provided tremendous inspiration for me as a young girl.

Jennifer, like Nana, felt compelled to share her story with others in hopes of inspiring empowerment. I met Jennifer because a woman named Meg O'Connell, who ran a foundation, referred me to Jennifer given her mission to empower women with breast cancer.

As I sat in Jennifer's driveway, I felt humbled by an overwhelming conviction that one day I, too, would be in a position to help empower women and give back to Jennifer's foundation in honor of my Nana. That day has arrived as this book will allow that dream to manifest itself. A portion of the proceeds from this book will be donated to Jennifer's nonprofit organization, Positively Pink Packages, in honor of my Nana.

Jennifer says, "What I neglected to realize in the beginning part of my journey to wellness is that acceptance of my condition was essential and knowledge was power. There wasn't a perfect answer as to 'why me?' Instead, I had to surrender to acceptance of my place in life, at that moment in time. My diagnosis made me realize that I could not control many aspects of my life."

Inspired Ideas for Daily Life

4. Surrender Your Worries.

Start a contemplative practice to help you be present in the moment and surrender your worries. Contemplative practices can include yoga, meditation or prayer. We can't control all the circumstances in our lives. The more we try to control every detail, the more we become frustrated by our lack of control.

Courage is Etched Inside of You

Eleanor Roosevelt said, "The future belongs to those who believe in the beauty of their dreams." Your future resides in your capacity to believe in yourself and aim for your dreams. Never let anyone tell you that you can't live out your dreams. Fear can hold us back in life but that is when we need to pull on our "big girl" pants and believe in ourselves. Together we can empower each other to soar and stretch our imaginations to accomplish the unimaginable.

In Jennifer's own words:

"The day I was diagnosed seemed to last forever. My once steady world felt as if someone had pushed me off a cliff with no preparation. I looked for ways to regain some semblance of control in my new world. Nothing felt 'normal.' I was just thirty-two years old!

The surgeon gently revealed that she had just received the pathology report, and the cancer had spread to my lymph nodes. After I pressed her, it was revealed that 15 of the 23 nodes were found to be positive for cancer. As I had a full week to become an expert on the subject of breast cancer, I asked if it had been detected in my blood. "Yes," my doctor replied. "If anyone can beat this, it's you" she continued, offering hope.

Sometimes in life, it's not until we are forced to wear a different pair of shoes that we realize how much we loved the comfort of the familiar ones. Maybe it's my slightly worn black clogs, rough around the edges with wide width that snuggled my foot, that I yearned for during the dark moments. However, my pink slippers, soft to the touch, became my new best friend.

After 33 radiation treatments, 16 weeks of chemotherapy, a partial hysterectomy, bilateral mastectomy and reconstruction, I worked to regain some semblance of normalcy and while undergoing treatment, began to formulate an idea that was close to my heart. While there was a good deal of information available for breast cancer patients, there weren't many resources or care packages to offer what I felt I could have used throughout my own recovery. I felt that women needed hope.

I channeled my personal experiences and designed Positively Pink Packages to inspire and offer hope at a time when women needed it most.

Recently, I shared my wit and wisdom at an event called Room Full of Sisters. At that moment, I realized how women have to passionately pursue their dreams, whether in the form of a business, organization or lifelong hobby, and that they need inspiration, hope and self-care to do so."

– Jennifer Tom

Inspired Ideas for Daily Life

5. Pursue Something With Passion.

Explore a new side of yourself. Take a pottery class or trek across new terrain. The community college or local community center is a great place to see what classes will be offered for a modest amount of money. I personally remember attending a romance writer's workshop for the first time in Phoenix. I found this experience helped me connect with interesting women writers.

Journal Writing Can Help

"The act of putting pen to paper encourages pause for thought. This in turn makes us think more deeply about life, which helps us regain our equilibrium." - Norbet Platt, writer

Studies show that the practice of journal writing provides a sense of well-being and other health benefits that include relief of physical stress (shown by lowered blood pressure), generally improved physical health, and a reduction in anxiety.

Mary Gardener, author of *My Life Matters-A Personal Record One Day at a Time,*[1] presented a copy of her book to me and shared the following: "It is in the activities of everyday life, the grand and the small, that we can find the realities of why our lives matter to us and to those we love. Unless we find some way to capture some of those memories, things we did, saw, thought about, felt or dreamed, we can forget them and lose

---

[1] MLMG Designs, 2005

the opportunity to enjoy them again, or reflect upon them, figure out why they matter to us."

Journal writing allows us to share feelings, chronicle life's moments, and find meaning in our daily occurrences. We can look within ourselves, gain perspective, and see our personal growth over time. There is no right or wrong method for writing in a journal; it's what works best for you.

Inspired Ideas for Daily Life

6. Write in bite-sized bits.

Become a word artist. Describe the sights and sounds, the tastes, the smells, the way things feel in your life. I found that pretty-colored journals that fit in my purse work best for me. When an idea, thought, or feeling arrives, I can capture the essence of the feeling, write it down and reflect on it later in the day.

Start Journaling

Although most bookstores sell elegant journals with leather covers and gold-edged pages, these can make journal writing seem like an impossible task. Inexpensive spiral notebooks or composition books allow you the freedom to be yourself. If you are anxious that someone will read your thoughts and writings without your consent, you may censor what you put on the page, which limits the benefits that writing provides. Be clear with others about your right to privacy.

What you share and what you keep to yourself is up to you. Often times, individuals save their writings in order to reread them or pass along. Others throw them away. The choice to keep or to discard your journal is also a personal one.

I remember as a teenager that my journal even had a key on it so my thoughts were private. I mostly wrote about my first kiss, my period and coming to terms with my adolescence. In college, I wrote poetry and stuck quotes that inspired me into my journal.

As I aged and life brought interesting challenges, I immediately returned to writing in my journal. I especially liked journals with colorful front covers and inspirational quotes printed throughout. You don't have to be a writer or an artist to keep a journal. There is a freeing action by releasing your thoughts and feelings on a piece of paper.

Inspired Ideas for Daily Life

7. Keep a Gratitude Journal.

Next to my bedside table is a journal marked gratitude. Here, I write my "thank you" list each morning. It takes just a few minutes to write down three things that I am grateful for in my life. The items change each day but the intention is the same: to give gratitude.

Pictures Inspire Us

Pictures can inspire us to think or dream bigger dreams. In a workshop that I hosted with Dr. Pamela Moss[2], the Soul Guide and a national speaker, she challenged participants to create a pictorial for the future; a living reminder of their power to manifest their dreams. We began the session by cutting out images from magazines of things, places or persons that inspired us, and placing these

---

[2] www.drpamelamoss.com

images onto poster board. At that time, I couldn't understand why my pictorial had many global images that appealed to me.

Immediately following the workshop, I placed that poster board in my office. Each day, I would look at it while I worked. Within a year, I was traveling internationally, meeting women who were living representations of the inspirational photos from my pictorial. It was in India that the light bulb moment arrived. I understood that I had co-created that moment, with women from various cultures.

Inspired Ideas for Daily Life

8. Collect Images to Visualize Your Dream.

Find an image or picture that inspires you and tape it to the inside of your journal, desk or bathroom mirror. As you stare at the picture, envision yourself in that moment. The more you look at this image, the more you will have an inspired reminder of something you want to reach.

Reflections for the Reader

A place for you to pen your thoughts and ideas or pause enough to notice your magnificence.

Food for Thought....

♥Jennifer's real life story inspires us to believe in the power of pursuing something with passion. What could you pursue at this stage in your life, to dream a bigger dream or do just for you?

Chapter 3
The Art of Self-Talk
Thought Affirmation

"We ask ourselves, who am I to be brilliant, gorgeous, talented and fabulous? Actually, who are you not to be?" – Marianne Williamson, spiritual teacher and bestselling author

"The thing you are ripening toward is the fruit of your life. It will make you bright inside, no matter what you are outside. It is a shining thing." – Stuart Edward White, American novelist

International author and workshop leader Dr. Susan Jeffers shares in her book, *Feel the Fear and Do it Anyway* "that no matter what degree of insecurity you are feeling, a part of you knows there is wonderful stuff within you just waiting to be let out and now is the perfect time for opening the door to the power and love within."[3]

Dr. Jeffers suggests a daily affirmation or phrase that provides positive reinforcement to you.

The concept of daily affirmations was a new idea for me. These thought patterns, repetitive words, mantras or phrases that include affirmations are much more popular now. I have personally experienced the benefits of using positive affirmations in my daily life. You control the thoughts that you implant in your mind. Even as you read this book, your thoughts are under your control.

You cannot change the past, but you can change your attitude of today and thus, your future.

Thoughts have a direct impact on our health. The more positive the images in our

---

[3] Vermillion, 20th Anniversary Edition 2007

minds, the healthier we will feel. For example, if a person repeatedly tells you it's going to rain, you will look outside and subconsciously expect rain versus sunshine.

Your self-perception operates in this manner. Just because someone tells you it's going to rain, using this example, doesn't mean you have to accept that as your own personal truth.

Negative self talk that leaks into our minds has a tendency to stay in our minds. If we repeat negative thoughts for a period of time, our minds begin to input data into our subconscious, influencing our self-perception. Each time I feel consumed by a negative thought, I tell myself to think positively. I would affirm for myself, by saying out loud, "today I am happy, healthy and grounded in joy".

Inspired Ideas for Daily Life

9. Surround Yourself with Empowering Words.

Find a quote that resonates with you. Select a word or phrase that has positive meaning. Play and replay that word or phrase like a song in your head when negative thoughts surface. Place an empowering quote in your purse or on your desk where you will see it daily.

Tell Yourself Today is a Great Day.

Positive self-talk is seeking out acceptance and love of self. Interestingly, I noticed negative self-talk increased my heart rate, caused anxiety and made me feel especially vulnerable.

Positive self-talk walked me toward inner peace and acceptance of myself. I designed a mantra to include in my affirmations, which is, "I believe and accept every inch of my beauty." Create one for you such as, "I choose to love myself and all of myself." Repeat it many times; the subconscious can be quite stubborn.

When the 14th Dalai Lama was asked, "What is it that makes me better?" he said, "Take care of your thoughts because they become your words. Take care of your words because they become your actions. Take care of your actions because they become your habits. Take care of your habits because they will form your character. Take care of your character because it will form your destiny, and your destiny will be your life. There is no religion higher than the truth."

Positive Self-Talk

"Nothing can dim the light that shines from within." – Maya Angelou, author, *I Know Why the Caged Birds Sing*

As I investigated attributes that make women flourish, I found a common thread in the positive power of intentions. One of my favorite inspirational writers is bestselling author Louise Hay, from whom I first discovered affirmations from her book, *You Can Heal Your Life*[4]. I put into practice what I read, and began to create my own affirmations. Louise says to continually make positive statements about how you want your life to be.

---

[4] Hay House, 1999

Always make statements in the present tense using, "I am," or "I have." Stating in the presence tense reinforces the mind. You will find that the more you repeat the phrase or affirmation, the psyche begins to accept this affirmation as truth. I found continuous behavior patterns can shift our energy.

My sample journal entry.....................

- ♥ I am living proof of creation.
- ♥ I am infinite beauty.
- ♥ I release all outdated beliefs.
- ♥ I understand that God helps me expand my consciousness to new areas of growth.

Forgiveness

"Forgiveness is the fragrance that the violet sheds on the heel that has crushed it." - Mark Twain, novelist

The past is over and done. You cannot change conditions and circumstances in the past. However, you can change your perception of it. The more you hold on to past wounds, the more you keep reliving the pain. Forgiveness is letting go of the past.

To release the past, we must be willing to forgive ourselves and let go of the negativity associated with the person who you feel wronged you. Yes, easier said than done.

Forgiveness starts in one's own heart. Forgiveness does not have to mean that you condone the situation or are ready to accept bad behavior. The fact that you are willing to forgive yourself is part of the healing process. Forgiveness is letting go.

Henri Nouwen in *Bread for the Journey*[5], a book of daily meditations, says, "To forgive another person from the heart is an act of liberation. We set that person free from the negative bonds that exist between us. We say, 'I no longer hold your offense against you.' But there is more. We also free ourselves from the burden of being the offended one."

---

[5] Harper Collins Publishers, 2006

We find in letting go of our internal anger, we open up our hearts to new possibilities. We then can shift our energy toward creation energy- spaces of energy where we want to reside and place our intentions.

Inspired Ideas for Daily Life

10. Write a Letter to Shed Any Past Hurts or Anger.

Instead of mailing or sharing the letter, burn it in a fireplace or fire pit. As you watch the ashes, say: "I forgive myself, I forgive all wrongs." If you need a friend with you for moral support, then gather a friend. The key is in letting go to make room for the new. I found this exercise quite freeing.

See Yourself as Amazing – Feel It and Believe It

"We become more adept at rising to the occasion each time we see ourselves doing it." – Sarah Ban Breathnach, author of the Simple Abundance series

Look closely in the mirror. Recognize that your true beauty lives within you. See the beauty of your inner spirit. You are amazing. Now take a few minutes to acknowledge to yourself a few amazing qualities that you possess. Don't claim what you don't have but instead see your talents, wisdom and beauty as God's creation as organic and integral to who you are.

First off, it is not ego centric to claim the God given talents that we have been given in life. Just the opposite, we honor our creator the most by recognizing our gifts and internal beauty.

I remember the first time as a teenager that I placed roller skates on my feet. I felt a surge of energy, so much that I wanted to roller skate all day long. A freedom by performing movement in motion. I felt wonderful. Then, I crashed down the huge hill in our neighborhood. However, I got back up and days later, went full speed with my roller skates on that hill again.

As an adult, when I hit final on the current version of this book, after a process of compilation of sticky notes, journal entries, inspired thoughts on pieces of paper- all placed in one central locale in a book form. Life's experiences probably could have said, quit. Yet this inner drive said, keep going.

One would say, is that tenacity or stupidity, as in the case of my teenage roller skating personal example? Well, what made me get up and try again was the fact that I looked in the bathroom mirror and had a self talk. I said, self, "I am going to step over fear. I loved that freedom of soaring in the wind, I can do this."

Now in the case of the book, during the writing process, many life changes, an ebb and flow occurred. It pushed me harder to believe in myself. I had to lean on my inner voice and believe that my intention of wanting to inspire another with stories and inspired lessons could in fact become reality.

Inspired Ideas for Daily Life

11. Mirror on the Wall.

Tape a 5x7 card on your bathroom mirror with positive affirmations. Mine reads: "I am extraordinary because God created me!

I am powerful and worthy of love, abundance and joy." Each morning, I look at the card and reinforce my belief system.

Mantras

A mantra is a word or phrase that is repeated. The word mantra originates from the Sanskrit word; "mantra" which means sacred utterance, word or groups of words thought to have a psychological and spiritual power[6]. Repetition of sounds engage the mind, can provide a clearing effect, and help one let go of negative energy. Mantras are phrases with intention.

Women who practice yoga shared with me that they do daily meditative prayer where they repeat key words or phrases. The words are repetitive in nature and have symbolic meaning. The more you say the words as part of your daily practice, the more you begin to believe the words. The words penetrate our psyche and help affirm our positive beliefs on a subconscious level.

---

[6] Jan Gonda, The Indian Mantra, Oriens, Vol. 16, pages 244-297.

Restore Balance in Your Life

I heard bestselling author and global speaker, Dr. Wayne Dyer lecture in San Diego at the "I Can Do It" Conference, and listened to how his life changing principles for harmonious living serve as a practical guide for restoring balance.

Dr. Dyer shares, "Your desire to be and live from greatness is an aspect of your spiritual energy. In order to create balance in this area of your life, you have to use the energy of your thoughts to harmonize with what you desire. Your mental energy attracts what you think about."

Imagine if each one of us made a conscious choice to be cultivators of positive intentions. The key to contentment comes from an internal state of peace. Love and kindness are directly connected to contentment. Be gentle with yourself.

If aspects of your life feel out of balance, take a look at how you can create harmony. Maybe it is as simple, as carving out 15 minutes a day, for just you. Walk, read a passage that inspires you or simply be still.

Inspired Idea for Daily Life

12. Find Catalysts for Empowerment.

Talk to a friend, mentor or someone you respect about what motivates them to think positive. Then write down for yourself that one quality. In my case, my mother and Nana have tenacity; a quality I greatly respect.

Power of Visualization

"The journey between what you once were and who you are now becoming is where the dance of life really takes place."- Barbara De Angelis, author, relationship and personal growth adviser

As I acquire life's wisdom, I recognize the beauty of nature in the stillness of God's green earth. For me, spring is a time of renewal. As a gardener, I look forward to fresh blossoms that arrive during springtime. Flowers that I have planted transform from bulbs to tulips. This act reminds me of transformation and how, like the tulip, we as women transform and bloom.

Tulip planting requires digging a hole deep enough in the earth during autumn, placing the bulbs in the ground, and covering them with soil. Usually by the time I am ready to plant the tulip bulbs, the ground is hard. I have to use my physical strength to dig the hole and plant the tulip. I visualize the color and height of the tulip, and hope that all my hard work will bring a future blossom.

Life is much like planting tulips. We must foster determination to plant beauty in our life. We must see that dormant times are opportunities to learn and expand our knowledge. For example, I use winter as a chance to read inspirational books, to journal, and to sketch out my garden ideas. I see past the dormancy to potential springtime blooms, both actual and metaphorical.

Inspired Idea for Daily Life

13. Visualize Your Dream.

Place sticky notes with positive sayings and images that speak to you about your dreams around your house.

My niece Sarah is a great example of believing and feeling a dream. She wanted to attend a private school that would open the doors to a great education. Academically, the school had high standards. Sarah believed in the power of dreams. She visualized herself at the school, walking the campus and believing in herself. She was accepted and was recently nominated for the President's Service Award for Community Excellence.

Reflections for the Reader

A place for you to pen your thoughts and ideas or pause enough to notice your magnificence.

Food for thought....

♥ In this chapter, there is a consistent theme of the power of visualization and using personal affirmations to envision goals or dreams. What is one affirmation that you could incorporate into your life, beginning with "I am?" And how could you form that sentence from a positive perspective?

Chapter 4
Sacred Spaces for Healing
Inner Wells of Light

"Your sacred space is where you can find yourself again and again." - Joseph Campbell, Author of *The Power of Myth*

"It is only by following your deepest instinct that you can lead a rich life and if you let fear of consequences prevent you from following your deepest instinct, then your life will be safe, expedient and thin."- Katharine Butler Hathaway, Author of *The Little Locksmith*

As part of my personal journey, sacred spaces became part of my life. A sacred space is a place where you can slow down to simply be. It may be a comfy chair with your favorite candle flickering next to you, or a place in nature where you can listen to the birds. The key to making a space sacred is nourishing your own inner spirit. As such, conceiving and integrating a sacred space into your daily life requires attention to your actions and attitude while in the sacred space.

My friend Erin gifted me her mother's antique chair. The fabric is slightly worn but comfortable, and it feels angelic to me. I have positioned the chair in the corner of my living room, and placed a basket of inspirational books next to it.

Inside the basket are a few of my favorite staples-a small pocket-sized book from my mother about St. Francis, a saint known for peace. There is an old edition of *Victoria* magazine, and *Fine Gardening* magazine with pictures of flowers and home spaces that inspire me to think about my own living space. I also keep a book on angels and my journal next to this chair, a sacred space.

My basket of staples may change over time but the same elements remain: a book with quotes to inspire me, and always a journal to pen my thoughts or ideas. A sacred space is a special space that you call your own. It is a place that inspires and nourishes you.

Inspired Idea for Daily Life

14. Create Sacred Spaces. Inspiration for Sacred Spaces could be...

♥ A particular chair in which to sit and read or write in a journal. A consistent space and known to family members as a special place that is yours and yours alone to just sit and be.

♥ A mat or blanket that can travel in your car. You can place the yoga mat in spaces of nature for inspiration and sit to observe sights and sounds around you.

♥ A closet inside your office where you can open the door and meditate to images and affirmative quotes that inspire.

Meditation

Author and spiritual teacher Elizabeth (I call her Beth) Wright[7] shared with me; "Peace and harmony can be found in meditation. Benefits of meditation include greater creativity, and decreased anxiety and depression; increased feelings of vitality and rejuvenation, and improved clarity of the mind."

Meditation has become part of Beth's lifestyle. She initially taught me the art of mediation. Beth would encourage me to sit still, focus on my breath and connect with my divine inner spirit. She told me it is in the stillness of sitting in a space with me that wisdom can arrive.

At first, the task of doing this practice felt awkward and my mind kept fixating on other things. Over time, five minutes of meditation grew to twenty minutes. I started to feel peace take over and fill in those areas of my mind and body that beckoned for it. Now, I can't image life without meditation.

---

[7] www.wrightspiritworks.com

Today, my meditation begins in a spot that I know will be serene and conducive to quiet contemplation. For me, if the weather is favorable, a natural setting provides the best atmosphere for meditation. My ideal location is outside on my side porch, alongside a pond garden.

On rainy days, I sit and meditate in the chair in my living room. I would recommend an environment away from disruptive noise where you can seek solitude.

As I sit in a cross-legged position, I breathe in to the count of three and exhale to the count of three for ten breaths. I make a conscious choice to breathe slowly and repeat a mantra. Our breath helps us to be centered and connect with our core center. In this cross-legged position, I find peace and inner nourishment for my spirit.

Being in a relaxed state brings forth fresh awareness. Fifteen minutes of meditation in the morning helps me start my day with contentment. I am then alert and grounded for the day. I feel an inner peace and am ready to tackle the day from a positive perspective.

Inspired Idea for Daily Life

15. Meditate.

Meditation can provide a tool for healing, self-awareness and spiritual development. I like to light a white candle during meditation. Deep breathe for five minutes while concentrating on a specific mantra such as "I AM LOVE".

Yoga as a Healing Tool

Georgia has a beautiful smile. After years of practicing yoga, she stumbled upon a 200-hour yoga teacher training called "Self-Awakening Yoga Teacher Training for Fifties-Plus." Inspired by the program's description, "There's no better time in life to begin developing your skills as a yoga teacher than when you are overflowing with the natural wisdom that comes with maturity," Georgia began training to become a yogi.

She shares "With new confidence in my ability, I listened to my inner teacher. Gradually deeper experiences and understanding of yoga emerged."

The Power of Prayer

"God does not take away trials or carry us over them, but strengthens us through them." – E.B. Pusey, British Theologian

If you are a spiritual person, you may want to try writing letters to God or your Higher Power in your journal. Many people find written prayer gives them comfort and solace during difficult times. Prayer can be as simple as quiet meditation or joining others in a congregation to pray.

If you open your mind to prayer, even if it begins with a white candle in your family room as you quietly recite, "I believe in something beside myself," you will feel tranquil.

The power of prayer is amazing if you give faith a chance. The universal power of prayer is independent of your religious upbringing, can lift the spirit, provide hope on the darkest day, and give you inspiration when all hope is lost. Take a chance and explore the supremacy of prayer.

A great read was sent to me for my booklist community. *The Miracle Chase*[8] is the story of three women, three miracles in their lives, and the power of faith through personal examples. These women were miracle chasers, some with more skepticism than others but on a path to prove that real life miracles exist in everyday life.

I love this part of the story: *"I laughed realizing that while chasing miracles had awakened a different relationship with God, the Miracle Chase had awakened a new relationship with each other. "*[9] Joan, one of the authors, is talking about her relationship with the co-authors. The point being that faith and the power of prayer brings us together in dialogue and helps us in our everyday lives.

Inspired Idea for Daily Life

16. Sit with a Prayer.

I find that St. Francis prayers invoke peace and are universal. The following is an excerpt from The Prayer of St. Francis,

---

[8] Sterling Ethos, 2010
[9] The Miracle Chase, Sterling Ethos, 2010

"Lord, make me an instrument of your peace. Where there is hatred, let me sow your love; Where there is injury, your pardon; Where there is friction, union; Where there is error, truth; Where there is doubt, faith; Where there is despair, hope; where there is darkness, light; where there is sadness, joy."[10]

Faith

According to women whose wisdom has been included in this book, faith was instrumental in helping them deal with the circumstances of change. When we are in flux, we should remind ourselves that faith is constant.

Dr. Marty Sullivan from Duke University School of Medicine believes that people who pray or meditate are more energetic and less likely to feel depressed. [11]

---

[10] Saint Francis of Assisi, His Essential Wisdom, Fall River, 2010, page 92

[11]groups.msn.com/heartlungtransplantsupportgroup/benefitsof prayer.msnw

Benefits of Prayer Include:

- ♥ A feeling of peace, inner contentment.
- ♥ Quite time for reflection.
- ♥ Hope in something beyond the self.

Healing Rituals

Rituals or ceremonies are present in our society and can be considered rites of passage. Some symbolize new life, such as the baptism of a young child where he or she is blessed with holy water. Rituals can help you deal with a loss of a loved one and provide a safe haven for expression of emotions.

Native American shamans still employ sand painting in elaborate healing practices, using powdered sandstone of different colors to paint sacred patterns that attract healing spirits. The patient sits on the painting while a chanting shaman invites the relevant forces to enter the painting and cure the patient. In the end, the sand is believed to have absorbed the negative forces, and is thrown away. [12]

---

[12] www.joyofritual.com

Rituals are a way to deal with loss, celebrate new experiences, and mark rites of passage. They can be daily routines or patterns that help us focus on the importance of a day. For example, taking a bath could be a ritual, to induce relaxation and calmness.

Journaling is another ritual, or always keeping a flower on your kitchen table that makes you happy is a ritual. If a ritual speaks to you, do it!

Rituals can range from:

- ♥ Journal writing for self-expression.
- ♥ Lighting a candle for new energy while quietly mediating.
- ♥ Dancing to music that enlightens the spirit.
- ♥ Planting a tree, flowering plant or symbol of loss that can show rebirth in nature.

Inspired Idea for Daily Living

17. Perform a Ritual.

Gather a few friends together, read an inspired poem, hold hands and celebrate life or rites of passage. In my groups, we burn a ceremonial candle and write positive intentions. Then we pass food around, have a glass of wine, and give honor for the blessings in our life.

Natures Healing Force

As a young girl, my mother encouraged me to pull the weeds, water the plants and sing to the robins in our family garden. My primary role was to tend to the raspberries, but it seemed that I was better at eating them than just picking them.

There was a creek behind the garden near my childhood house, where water flowed freely and represented movement in nature. Life forces gathered for a little drink during those hot summer days. The creek was enjoyed by wildlife. As a teenager, I neglected to appreciate nature as a healing force and an energy that helps a person feel rejuvenated. I have come to value that the sheer act of seeing things alive reinforces that nature has new beginnings.

A flower, bird or tree can inspire a person to be present and be filled with a renewed sense of perspective by watching all that nature has to offer. In nature, there is living proof that things sprout new growth. Much like human beings, they bloom and blossom.

Inspired Idea for Daily Living

18. Be Present in the Moment.

Sit in silence for fifteen minutes in a place of nature, and observe your surroundings. Notice a bird in flight, the green grass or a stream. Just be present.

Gardening

Planting, digging the earth soil, and seeing something grow is an amazing feeling. The natural infrastructure of the earth gives a person a sense of grounding. Try simple things like planting tulip bulbs in a pot or growing tomato plants. You could even plant a rose bush somewhere in the yard or in a planter box in your apartment; then you truly will be inclined to "stop and smell the roses!"

Inspired Idea for Daily Life

19. Surround Yourself with Things that are Alive.

Grow indoor blooming plants on your nightstand or desk. I love my blooming cactus plant on my nightstand. Harvest life in your home with living, breathing things.

Reflections for Readers

A place for you to pen your thoughts and ideas or pause enough to notice your magnificence.

Food for Thought......

♥In this chapter, the concept of ceremonial rituals is introduced. What life events, accomplishments or rites of passage, could you perform as a ceremony for yourself? What would that ceremony look like? Why not invite over a friend to share in your personal journey?

Chapter 5
Take Time for Yourself
Image the Possibilities

"To keep a lamp burning, we have to keep putting oil in it." - Mother Teresa, Nobel Peace Prize recipient

"There is a place deep in your soul where a little seed rests. This seed is your amazing potential. Each time you push yourself, each time you breathe a true deep breath, each time you reach your hands to the stars, you nourish that little seed and feed your soul." – Karen Tye, Christian author

According to the National Women's Health Information Center,[13] women should make time for themselves by setting aside at least fifteen minutes a day to manage stress. The opportunity to carve out time in one's day isn't that easy for many women so this may seem a daunting task at first.

Many of us are all things to all people, but rarely take time for ourselves; however, once you get into a routine of self-care it becomes natural. Personally, I have found that self-care involves healthy food choices, a sacred space, contemplative practices and walks in nature, or surrounding me with living things.

Getting Comfortable with Me

"A day dawns quite like other days; in it, a single hour comes quite like other hours; but in that day and in that hour the chance of a lifetime faces us." – Maltbie Babcock, clergymen and writer of 19th century

---

[13] www.nia.nih.gov

My first real trip by myself was to a wellness center, Miraval Resort and Spa in Tucson, Arizona. I had been on many trips prior, both for work or with family and friends, but this was my first trip alone. As I arrived, the desert foliage was in full bloom.

The lodging was made up of adobe-like casitas with red roofs, and stucco and clay based motifs. There was a particular energy infused throughout this majestic oasis where the air was crisp, and nature through the mountains in the background of the desert landscape evoked peaceful harmony.

I brought a journal and the bare necessities on this trip. Self-awareness told me that I had to peel back the layers of my emotional self, let go of limited beliefs and be present in the moment. Quietly each morning, in the Catalina Mountains, I wrote in my journal.

My journal entries began with:

"I focus my energy on letting go of all which does not serve me well and embracing what the universe has planned for me. "

Self-care was a dramatic shift for me, since I had learned early on, to put the needs of others ahead of my own. Initially, I felt guilty- I had to give myself permission to take care of myself!

As the sun set, I walked inside a circular path of rocks known as a labyrinth, with my hands in prayer position. I asked my own inner spirit to guide me. At first, my ego was winning. It was telling me how I could improve myself, instead of guiding me toward self-acceptance. There was a kiva (fire pit) where I threw in a piece of paper written with all my limited beliefs. My list was long, built from years of self-criticism and self-imposed expectations for achievement.

Nevertheless, I was willing to mentally say "yes" to a life of creation.

I claimed my birthright as one of God's creatures to be my authentic self. I wrote, in all capitals: "I am worthy of love, abundance and happiness."

Today, I see life with eyes wide open and have learned that the little things we do in our everyday lives that make us pause and take notice, reside inside us. We don't need to venture far away to look within. We are similar. Each of us can sit on a rock, in a rocking chair or outside on a bench in nature to slowly and gently release our limiting beliefs.

We can put our energy in motion; our thoughts and self-perceptions formulate our day. Instead of focusing on what's not working in your life, direct your thoughts toward positive intentions.

The lesson is that attitude dictates our day. You may feel overwhelmed at times, but you can shift your attention to mindful living. Let go of all worries and envision yourself feeling a positive light in your life. Witness the small blessings in your life. Feel your own breath. Carve out time in each day for self care.

Inspired Idea for Daily Living

20. Do One Thing Every Day That Makes You Happy.

That one thing could be as simple as pouring yourself a cup of tea or coffee and reading your favorite newspaper at the onset of each day. Or turn on your favorite song in the car, as you drive to work.

Balanced Living

Chris Pulito is passionate about health. I first met Chris, when he was the resort manager for a wellness center in my home town, the Mirbeau Inn & Spa. As a nutrition educator and former competitive skier who blew out his knee and subsequently went through rehabilitation to gain mobility; Chris knows firsthand the positive effects of healthy life choices.

Chris shared with me: "The critical elements to a healthy lifestyle are everything in moderation with balance. If you fall off the bandwagon, don't give up. Get back on track the next day. Treat yourself with a disciplined approach. If you have a piece of chocolate cake for dinner, the next day eat a fruit- filled breakfast, fish for dinner, and exercise for thirty minutes."

Chris continued: "Healthy living has a direct correlation with happiness. When the body is healthy, a person gets sick less often, feels better about him or herself, has a heightened level of accomplishment and as a result, their quality of life is enhanced."

Inspired Idea for Daily Living

21. Everything in Moderation.

Be gentle with yourself. If you eat cake, then take a walk. If you overdo it on the caffeine one day, try drinking water the next day instead. In my case when out to dinner with friends, I split my dinner in half. I eat half of what is on my plate and take the other half home for my lunch the next day.

Healthy Habits

A great way to release tension in the body, and a proven avenue for better health, is exercise. When you are harboring negative thoughts, go for a walk. If you'd like to lift weights but don't have any, lifting soup cans is a great substitute. When I am devoted to my exercise routine, I feel a sense of accomplishment. Any built up stress subsides.

Exercise can free the mind and allow the blood to flow in a positive direction. If you lack the energy, set minor goals such as a fifteen-minute walk. During the winter months, my free weights come in handy. My physician told me to walk briskly 20 minutes a day, every day: "Exercise releases the endorphins, allows muscles to work efficiently and stimulates feelings of mental wellness."

Inspired Idea for Daily Life

22. Add Movements to Your Routine.

When my friend and walking partner, Shelly, was injured in a skiing accident, she took up rowing. The act of rowing strengthened her back, and over time she became a competitive rower, winning a gold medal for US Masters Rowing with teammates. She set small and manageable goals, surpassed personal expectations, and loved the friendships she formed with the rowing team.

Stress Soothers

Stress can build up over time or arrive quickly and furiously. It can manifest itself in the form of body aches, sleep deprivation or a general tension in the body. People respond differently to stress, depending on the type of stimuli, past ingrained behaviors from childhood and life's conditions. The more one retains stress, the greater the impact on the mind and body.

The key to healthy living is to focus on reducing stress and finding ways to manage it.

One way to soothe stress is to immerse yourself in a relaxing environment. Sit on a park bench and listen to the sounds of nature to ignite positive feelings. Create an atmosphere for yourself and light a scented candle (lavender and chamomile are known for relaxing properties) and play relaxing music to aid you in achieving a relaxed state.

Inspired Idea for Daily Life

23. Engage in Relaxation Activities.

An author friend of mine who lives in New Mexico goes to hot springs where she boosts her immune system and relaxes. I find the simple pleasures like filling up my own bathtub with lavender essential oil, lighting a sandalwood candle and playing spa-like music works great.

The Power of Breath

"Just breathe. Ten tiny breaths…Seize them. Feel them. Love them." – K.A. Tucker, *Ten Tiny Breaths*

Breathing is the easiest, cheapest form of therapy. Deep breathing can release tension, create tranquility and improve the body's response to environmental conditions. The most effective way is to breathe deeply and slowly.

Deep breathing invites oxygen into our bodies and rids the body of toxins. The type of breathing we are more familiar with tends to be shallow and quick, especially since we move so fast in our daily lives.

Becoming more aware of your breath is easy. Place your hand on your diaphragm, right above your belly button. Breathe in to the count of three (slowly) and exhale to the same count. Notice your hand moving up and down as you breathe and release air. If you focus on your ability to slowly inhale and exhale, you can release stress.

I came to recognize that when I sit still, my heart opens up to the possibility that each day holds for me. The more I am connected with myself, the easier the day flows. I am alert and ready to be present in the flow of energy. Any worries float away. I am simply present in the moment.

Inspired Idea for Daily Life

24. Focus on Your Breath.

Sit in a comfortable position. As you inhale, picture yourself drawing in clean, crisp ocean air and feel your lungs filling up. Count to three as you inhale clean air in your lungs. Then as you exhale, imagine all the stress and tension flowing out of your body, and the ocean washing over you with clean, fresh air.

Happiness is Your Birthright

I first met women's wellness instructor and Kundalini yoga teacher, Bonita Shear[14] when she taught breath walking.

Bonita says: "When your spirit is filled with light and doing the things you enjoy, everything else falls into place. You are in the flow. Whatever stage you are in during your life span, always find a slice of time for you. Be good to yourself. Be your own best friend. Never feel guilty for taking time for you."

Bonita imparts wisdom by showcasing that she practices what she preaches. She shares: "My daily life and practices keep me grounded and in balance. I start my day by setting the stage for a positive and happy day. Before my feet hit the ground, I repeat a

---

[14] www.bonitaiam.com

powerful affirmation that pertains to a change that I want to make in my life."

Bonita's personal affirmation is, "The universe is a giant sounding board."

Inspired Ideas for Daily Life

25. Walk with Purpose.

The sheer act of walking with gratitude invokes a positive feeling, and makes the day seem purposeful.

26. Create a daily routine where you take time to just be in a contemplative state.

This state could involve sitting and just being present in the moment by yourself, and allowing stillness to pour forth. You could recite a prayer, read a passage in a book or just sit still.

Laughter is Medicine For the Soul

As Norman Cousins, author of *Anatomy of an Illness*[15] discovered, "When you laugh, endorphins-the body's natural painkillers- are released." Too many times in life, we forget the power of simple and accessible experiences such as laughter. Having a healthy sense of humor can make life more rewarding and manageable.

Children's laughter is infectious, especially when they are mesmerized by things that most adults overlook. When I think of my five-year-old twin nephews, I laugh. One of the twins, Paulie, recently spent a week with my parents. He was obsessed with my dad taking him fishing at the trout stream.

Paulie sat on a plastic bucket, wearing his jean shorts and fish T-shirt, his miniature fishing pole by his side. In that moment, you couldn't help but hope he caught "the big one that got away," as my father would say about the clever fish that teased and then swam the other way.

---

[15] Norton, W. W. & Company, Inc, 2005

On one particular day, Paulie reeled in "the one that got away." The fish was longer than the length of Paulie's outstretched arms. We had many great laughs that day and I realized how children, with their simple enjoyments, can make us laugh. When we are present with a child, and do activities, we acquire a sense of enjoyment.

Healing Circles

Community provides a sense of wellbeing and togetherness. We know that there is something uniquely common to be shared with other women. We are mothers, grandmothers, and creative spirits that have overcome challenges in our life.

Women like to gather together and share personal stories. When I was a child growing up in an Italian household, we would congregate in the kitchen. It was a focal point of gatherings. Here, generations of aunts, cousins and sisters spent time playing Gin Rummy or Crazy Eights while the eldest cooked homemade sauce.

Each of us would taste the sauce on a piece of Italian bread as the day progressed. We would offer our comments—perhaps a little hot pepper, a little more salt, put the pork sausage in now—and laugh, cry or share a tidbit of our week.

As I have aged and watched loved ones pass, the memories of our special times serve as inspiration for new times. Now, we gather in my sister's kitchen with her boys, the cousins and the aunts to create new memories.

My mom said to me, "There is family in a great pot of sauce. No matter how the sauce tastes, we have the bond that brings us together-our roots and experiences for the next generation to witness. We can laugh, cry, express ourselves but there is a sense of community."

Inspired Idea for Daily Life

27. Gathering Circles Around the Table.

Break bread with family and friends. Host a potluck dinner and share life tales.

Gather with a pot of soup and a bottle of good wine; play cards. Take pictures so you have memories to share with future generations.

Reader Reflections

A place for you to pen your thoughts and ideas or pause enough to notice your magnificence.

Food for Thought......

♥The concept of taking daily time for oneself, even fifteen minutes is emphasized in this chapter, as well, as community gatherings. How could you carve out some time for yourself? Could you start today to allocate some time to nourish your mind, body and spirit?

Chapter 6
The Power Within
Let Peace Begin with Me

"People are like stained glass windows: they sparkle and shine when the sun is out, but when the darkness sets in their true beauty is revealed only if there is a light within." – Elizabeth Kubler-Ross, author, *On Death and Dying*

"If we could see the miracle of a single flower clearly, our whole life would change."- Buddha, spiritual teacher

Empowerment lives inside of each one of us. Sometimes, we do not understand our ability to be strong until we are called to be strong. Too many times in life, we let the negative experiences dictate our future. Our greatest power exists in our inner strength-a grace that comes from within.

Recently I had the chance to meet with Noelle, a 10-year-old from Central New York. Noelle has shoulder- length hair, a noble smile and a certain unspoken charm. As we visited, her mother, Ingrid, sat alongside us. I saw the love in Ingrid's eyes as she watched her daughter test her sugar level using a kit that modern technology suggests is advanced sugar flux detection for a Type 1 diabetic.

Noelle was diagnosed with Type 1 diabetes at nineteen months old, coupled with a later diagnosis of celiac disease. This complicated life for Noelle and her family, as they need to be hyperaware of the food Noelle eats.

Despite extensive monitoring, Type 1 diabetes in children her age is hard to regulate. Since Noelle's diagnosis of Type 1 diabetes, she's had 17,000 insulin injections and has tested her blood more than 30,000 times.

As I look at my healthy 10-year-old nephew, I can't imagine him stopping what's he's doing to test himself eight to ten times a day for sugar changes in his body. This concept seemed impossible to me until I met Noelle. This young girl educated me.

Noelle presented me with a beautiful picture as a token of gratitude for the gift of my time. I saw God's presence in the world etched inside of her. I am certain that Noelle will help teach others through education, interaction with her service dog named Dulce, and her own empowering actions.

Lessons Learned from an Inspiring Encounter:

- ♥ Believe-there is a lesson to be learned every day.
- ♥ Exhibit grace under pressure. To find inner strength when we are tired, call upon that strength.
- ♥ Celebrate the little moments in life that bring joy.

Inspired Idea for Daily Life

28. Gratitude is Attitude.

As you start the day, recognize three things you are grateful for in this life. When I practice gratitude, the power of intention is established at the onset of a day and my energy tends to be more positive.

Let Peace Begin with Me

"If we have no peace, it's because we have forgotten that we belong to each other. " – Mother Teresa

When I hosted a book launch party for *IHood: Our GPS for Living* by Dr. Jill Little,[16] I had a certain anxiety. Jill was my mentor, a professor of philosophy, and a personal friend, and this book was the accumulation of her life's work. Stricken unexpectedly by a brain aneurysm, Jill died and left behind her writings-the makings of a sixth book. The day of her book signing, I sat in my office chair

---

[16] Pegasus Books, 2013

and prepared my speaking p
asking for inspiration from a
thought about Jill's role in m
rang in my head, "Be an inst
she had said.

Jill Little lived her life   , ...p.., ...
of compassion and a conviction to inspire
others. She would hold the hands of readers
in workshops, listening to their personal
stories and always offering encouragement.
Jill would say, "It is our ego which makes us
believe we aren't good enough, but it is our
spirit which says we were formed for
greatness."

I learned from Jill that circumstances
in life are not always easy; that we must find
the inner strength to press ahead and believe
that we can make a difference in the world.

On the day of the book launch party, I
wrote my speech: "All peace first begins
within the heart space. We can search for all
external happiness, but true peace lives inside
of us. The battle between the ego (our mind)
provides a fruitless existence; material things
just fill up space. Spiritual paths ignite the
light, and the light spreads. Instead, it's time

our energy toward abundance, ernal joy and harmonious living!

It's time to make a conscious choice to claim all that lives within us, God's presence. In this moment, take time to quietly own the path to peace–to be still, to be present in our daily living. For parents to embrace each quality of their child, to nurture creativity and to teach self care.

In this moment, know that all love begins with self-love, a concept that is foreign to many of us. Self-love means self worth with compassionate living. Be kind to yourself. Take time to embrace all of life's experiences."

Words from an Enlightened Being

When the 14th Dalai Lama spoke at Cornell University in October 2007, he said that the key to joyful living first originates with peace within the individual. Five thousand chairs were packed together like sardines, as all eyes fixated on the Dalai Lama. Tibetan monks chanted in their native language while in their robes.

I viewed the entire event via simulcast broadcast and recalled that the atmosphere was majestic. A Tibetan bell rang and seemed to set the tone for prolific moments of enlightenment. An infectious smile with a boisterous laugh highlighted the stature of a man clothed in a garment that reminded me of the color of a deep profuse sunset. The 14th Dalai Lama sat cross-legged.

You could hear a pin drop in the room as all eyes were on 14th Dalai Lama when he said "Take time to be quiet, remain optimistic and have self-confidence."

Perform Acts of Kindness

My mom taught me at a young age that servitude to others brings great joy. As a young girl, I would volunteer at church activities, raise funds for church repairs through candy bar sales and serve with Girl Scouts of America. However, I preferred my roller skates, my Jordache jeans, best friends, and my rock and roll music in my room to random acts of kindness. It was indeed an effort, as a young child, to learn the value of living in service to others.

The Random Acts of Kindness Foundation,[17] an organization committed to encouraging kind action, states that health benefits associated with acts of kindness increase our sense of self-worth; provide greater happiness and optimism, as well as, a decrease in feelings of helplessness and depression.[18]

When I was around seven years old, I would play for hours with my Barbie Dreamhouse. My sister and I dreamed up excursions for Barbie, Ken and Barbie's best friend, Midge. Our imaginations ran wild. On nice days, we gathered the dolls, Dreamhouse, and all its contents, and ventured outside to the creek where we camped in nature.

I absolutely loved Barbie.

Imagine my shock when during a family garage sale, my mother told us to pack up Barbie, her friends, and the Dreamhouse, and

---

[18]Random Acts of Kindness Foundation, www.actsofkindness.org

give all of it to a little girl at our garage sale. Despite our resistance, we gathered everything and placed contents in a plastic bag, and handed everything over to the young girl. She was ecstatic.

Her brother grabbed Ken and said, "Mama, I'm going to be like Ken someday, tall with a Dreamhouse." My mom refused any payment and placed a religious statue in the bag as well. In that moment, I learned the meaning of "random acts of kindness." My Mom told me that God wants us to share whatever we had with other boys and girls. She said, "It's in giving that we receive much more from the sheer act of sharing."

Inspired Idea for Daily Life

29. Perform Random Acts of Kindness.

Take a meal to a sick or elderly neighbor, volunteer at a soup kitchen, do something for someone else in need with no expectation of a return gift. For it is in giving to others that we receive many blessings.

Today is Your Birth Day

Each moment is a new beginning. Remember, you are the only one responsible for the thoughts in your own head. Imagine if you embraced today as a birthday. "Today is my birthday. I celebrate the moments of my life, when all things are well." Begin your day with the belief that today is your birthday and a celebration of you.

A New Beginning

"Every day is a fresh new beginning,
Listen my soul to the glad refrain
And, spite of old sorrows
And older sinning,
Troubles forecasted
And possible pain,
Take heart with the day, and begin again."
-Susan Coolidge, American children's author[19]

---

[19] The Times of London, www.thetimes.co.uk

Inspired Idea for Daily Life

30. Surround Yourself with Happiness Objects.

Examples might include a picture of your son or daughter as the home screen on your cell phone or computer, a ruby red flower, or a picture of your favorite memory. Any image that makes you happy.

Count Your Blessings

Keep an account of the good things in your life. Write down your daily blessings such as a glorious sunrise, a smile from a stranger, or a letter from a friend.

Acknowledge Your Blessings

Acknowledge out loud or write down five blessings in your life and place this list in a place where you will see it daily to serve as an inspirational reminder for you.

My blessing list is as follows:

I am grateful for my breath, this nature haven, my dog, Bunny, all my God- given talents through lessons learned, and my family.

Inspired Ideas for Daily Life

31. Create a Blessings List.

Write down your blessings on a piece of paper, in your journal, or in an email to someone in your life. Share your gift of truth with another. Too often we overlook the people in our lives who mean the most.

Ability to Envision the Future

Your outlook for tomorrow dwells in your ability to envision the future. Perseverance and positive thinking will be the catalyst that enables you to *Live the Life of Your Dreams*. Every experience large or small, comfortable or uncomfortable makes us grow. Our ability to envision the future begins with self perception. See yourself as amazing and know that you were formed for a unique purpose.

All life experiences make you who you are today, and even our hardest times serves as catalysts for growth and new perceptions.

Start your day by envisioning yourself in a positive mode. I found it helpful to place images of inspiration around me, a pictorial for the future. These images include places I wanted to visit and book cover images for my upcoming books-so I could see them and believe them. Each day, I would take a few minutes to look at these images and envision them as reality.

You are the Only Artist who can Paint Your Own Landscape

Comparable to an artist, you make a choice to paint or draw your life the way you want it to be. Self-expression comes in different colors and with brushstrokes that vary in color. Some of us choose to paint a canvas with dark colors, while others choose vibrant colors. The common element here is that we all have the ability to create the picture in our life.

Set small manageable steps so you can rejoice when you achieve them. Use the space in the **Reader Reflections** to get started in defining your landscape painting. For example, I want to celebrate my forty-third birthday a year from now with people that mean the most to me.

Women Share their Landscape Paintings:

- ♥ A trip to Italy before her husband passed on.
- ♥ A trip with the grandkids to Disney World.
- ♥ Exploring one's creative side with a pottery class.
- ♥ Walking in *Relay for Life*, after surviving cancer.
- ♥ Publishing my works of poetry, which I did.

Reader Reflections

A place for you to pen your thoughts and ideas or pause enough to notice your magnificence.

Food for Thought......

♥ As the artist of your own personal painting, what would your landscape painting look like? What are your dreams? How could you direct your attention toward creating reality for a landscape painting?

Chapter 7
Live Life with Passion
Dare to Dream

"May you be truly blessed to always glitter with a radiance that shines from deep within you." -Barbara Becker Holstein, positive psychologist and originator of Enchanted Self series

"If you were all alone in the universe with no one to talk to, no one with which to share the beauty of the stars, to laugh with, to touch, what would be your purpose in life? It is the other life; it is love, which gives your life meaning. This is harmony. We must discover the joy of each together, the joy of challenge, the joy of growth." -Mitsugi Saotome, author of *Aikido and The Harmony of Nature*

Sometimes, in order to be happy, you have to stay in the present moment instead of worrying about yesterday or tomorrow. I once heard that the best prediction of happiness is happiness now.

Happiness can be a litmus test, given to the human condition at times; the litmus test will show different things-joy, sorrow, excitement, disappointment, love. I have learned that true happiness starts from within. A person, thing, or job can't provide happiness because happiness is a feeling of union with the self.

As I walked the path removing limitations from my life and shifting my energy to co-create, creating the Life of my Dreams, I began to understand the power of self-love.

Instead of punishing yourself for past mistakes, learn from your past. Every experience offers a lesson, even the most challenging times. Factors that influence our happiness include childhood experiences, genetic makeup, and the ability to be in union with the self and a higher power. This book is about creating a life that empowers one to think bigger, and provides inspirational tools to reach that goal.

Part of acquiring happiness involves compassionate understanding. When we send out good intentions and serve others, we receive energy that magnifies us. Women who have overcome challenges share the path of happiness laid in forgiveness of self and others. When they expanded their consciousness to living a life with purpose, their daily lives brought joy.

Dare to Dream

"We are God's gift to us. What we become is our gift to God." – Eleanor Powell, American film actress of 1930s and 1940s

I remember the desire to learn something new, to surround myself with like-minded people and to expand my creative side.

As I look back in my journal, I see questions like:

♥ *If anything at all were possible, quickly, easily and began today, what would your life look like? Who would be in your life and how would you spend your time?*

♥ *Your inner voice knows all the answers. Imagine if one year from now, you have been able to create everything you have always dreamed. What would it take?*

I challenge you to think about these questions. Write down some creative ideas in response to these questions in your journal or on a piece of paper. Have dialogues with close friends, family members, or work mentors about your thoughts to these questions. Recognize that you can with baby steps or large leaps of faith-create the *Life of Your Dreams.*

In my own life, I made a conscious decision to meditate each morning for twenty minutes. I then practice yoga poses for another fifteen minutes. I practice this daily and when guests come to stay, I simply state that I am in meditation.

As a business owner, I devised operating principles or what I call "rules of engagement," for like-minded people. When I consider taking on a client, I review my rules of engagement to achieve conscience-building practices, before committing to project engagement. I realized that socially, my desire is to spend time with like-minded people who value service to others. In that decision, some of my friendships have faded away but God has brought me new, enhanced friendships.

I made a healthy decision to take three days for just me every few months. If I want to stay in my pajamas, I do so. If I want to go to a wellness spa, I do it- guilt-free.

My Life Compass

As part of creating my own pictorial for life, my life compass has been guided by the following principles:

- ♥ Surround yourself with like-minded people.
- ♥ Stay true to yourself.
- ♥ Expand your horizons by being open to new experiences.
- ♥ Take on work projects that invigorate or allow you to flex your creative muscles.

♥ Claim abundance. For example, "The more I make, the more I can help others." (Note: Abundance is much more than monetary worth. Friends, family, and special moments are worth more than a pot of gold.)

When discussing the concept of empowerment with women, some limiting beliefs included a lack self-worth, past mistake guilt, relationship setbacks and financial security, or lack thereof.

Women who take more risks shared that they had one "support champion" in their life-a friend or family member who encouraged them to think bigger.

Inspired Idea for Daily Life

32. Discover Your Support Champions.

Surround yourself with positive reinforcement; a monthly cup of tea or lunch with a friend can do wonders for empowerment. Women can support each other's goals. Men can be great support champions as well, especially as mentors in the business world and as life partners.

The 5X7 Card

Four-time Olympian and award winning speaker Ruben Gonzalez wrote in his book, *The Courage to Succeed,*[20] that "hope accomplishes the impossible." Ruben is a great example of an individual with an immense power of belief.

At 21 years old, Ruben decided that he wanted to become an Olympic winner and took up luging. Most people had more than ten years of experience, while Ruben had zero. He did not listen to his fears or to the people who said he could not reach that level of success. Instead, he trained and developed a passion for achieving success.

Ruben wrote out on a 5X7 index card his dream of winning a gold medal, and each day he read his reminder. His power of belief helped him achieve Olympic status. His beliefs include achieving greatness: "Great people are not born. They become great by

---

[20] Aspen Press, 2004

making a decision to pursue their dream in life and by refusing to give up. The struggle we must all face on the road to our dreams is what makes us great. Ordinary people can become extraordinary if they dedicate their lives to the pursuit of happiness."[21]

While I agree in principle with Ruben's commentary, I challenge his concept of extraordinary. I believe we were formed as an extension of God, and therefore are indeed born extraordinary. What we do with those God-given talents is up to us. As my mother would say, "You can lead a horse to water, but the horse must choose to drink."

A successful friend of mine, a CEO of a business marketing research firm, shared that he had a sign on a bookcase in his college dorm that read: "Quit not me." These three words inspired him when he was getting ready for his college football games, studying for a test, or later in life in the business world, to never give up. These words empowered him to dream bigger dreams and served as a simple yet constant reminder of his life philosophy.

---

[21] Ruben Gonzalez, www.thelugeman.com

You Create the Picture of Your Life

My friend Mary gave me a great Christmas gift, a sign that says, "Life is Art, Paint Your Dreams." This gift was symbolic because we discussed especially in times of uncertainty, that we had the power to paint our landscape like we envisioned it. As I spoke with women about the topic of this book, they shared that their landscape paintings had changed, been modified or needed an update. Some women felt that work, kids and marriage made their priorities shift, and the concept of self care and dreaming a bigger dream, seemed really far off in the distance. Like an unfathomable concept.

Yet, I challenge you to realize that you alone can create an ideal pictorial. You deserve a life in balance. If you are unhappy with the picture of your life, then take the steps necessary to modify your picture. If you like the picture, ensure you are working toward maintaining or enhancing that picture. Remember, you are the only artist who can paint your canvas any way you envision.

You Have the Power of Choice

My client and award-winning author, Sheila Applegate, of *Enchanted One: A Portal to Love*,[22] inspires others in her workshops. Sheila encourages people to make room for miracles. She says, "In every moment, you have a choice: love or fear, unity or separation. We can choose limited beliefs of fear, thinking that we are separate from our source or Creator, or we can choose to embrace all that is within us, God's creation."

We can see ourselves as worthy of experiencing joy in our daily lives or we can look at our lives with a limited belief system. Limited beliefs can include, "I am not worthy," "I need more now," "I am a victim of my past."

If we shift the part of our mind that keeps replaying old outdated tapes, we can turn our attention to, "I am worthy of love." An example of this shift is to truly believe in the following statement: "I live in the present moment. The universe supports me now."

---

[22] Turning Stone Press, 2012

Shifting mindsets takes time, and repetition. Like a muscle we would shape, our psyche is the same- we must nourish, shape and acknowledge the part of our internal markup where beauty and confidence reside.

Some self-destructive beliefs are stubborn. I have discovered that to overcome these beliefs, the repetition of positive affirmations is essential. In my case, I select a twenty-one day affirmation. Every day for twenty-one days, I convinced myself of my worthiness. As a result, I started to see a shift in my dreams, in acquired abundance, and in inner peace.

I began to believe that I was worthy of abundance in my life in all forms. Gratitude became a daily practice. Creation energy engulfed me and a conscious shift toward joy in each day.

What if? - Some things to ponder

♥ You wrote affirmations in your journal that state your worthiness?

- ♥ You shifted your conscious thinking to stepping over fear-based thoughts toward positive thinking?
- ♥ What if you started today?

As I look back to what I penned in my journal, I see that words entailed:

My Affirmation

Dear God,

I am worthy of love. Today in this moment, I am going to walk hand in hand with you. I am going to trust in my belief that I am extraordinary. That formed in creation energy, I can claim my inner power to live a healthy life. In every moment, I see my inner beauty as a reflection on this Earth. I am woman. I am divinity. I am powerful. I am peace and love. I claim all my infinite worthiness today. I completely surrender and trust in all that is infinite in this moment.

We Become What We Believe About Ourselves and Others

"Beauty appears when something is completely and absolutely and openly itself."- Deena Metzger, storyteller and novelist

How do we find the power within to create an inspired life?

- ♥ Surround yourself with at least one symbol of hope.
- ♥ Practice positive self-talk.
- ♥ Take care of yourself. The more we have a healthy mind and body, the more we can live an inspired life.

Harmonious Spaces

When my marriage ended, I felt the need to create a new harmonious space with cans of paint and repurposed furniture. I selected a new color for my bedroom. It was a color that really spoke to me-a soothing light blue color to remind me of the sky and which also had a spa-like feel. I placed plants in the light, and rearranged the furniture.

I surrounded myself with images that inspired me: My Nana's statue of the Virgin Mary, a small painting of a woman standing next to a creek, and a blooming cactus plant. I felt new energy in the room. The redesign of the space extended into other living areas of my house as well. I set up sacred mini-spaces for myself: a chair surrounded by plants and books for inspiration. I also created conversation spaces for visits with friends and family.

Soon, I extended my harmonious living plans to my outside space. I decided to declutter my life. I packed up household items for donation, including many life trinkets, which no longer served a purpose. With a mantra of *simplification* I felt more at ease with less stuff, and more meaning in my everyday life.

This practice opened up the recognition of the following:

- ♥ You cannot take a U-Haul to Heaven.
- ♥ There is great joy in having less, giving more meaning in our belongings.

♥ Sitting in a space of stillness, where we turn off the noise, if even for a few minutes a day quiets the soul and allows inner knowledge to pour forth.

Inspired Idea for Daily Life

33. Create Harmonious Living Spaces.
Grab a can of paint, and paint a wall with a color that speaks to you. Place items in the room that inspire you. Include living plants, images, and books that can help create a place of inspiration. Simplify all of your clutter, remove things that are not necessary in your life and donate them to a cause that is close to your heart.

Rebirth

Rebirth is a process whereby one rediscovers life in a new form, a new direction, or way of spending one's time. Enlightenment can arrive at strange times and unexpectedly. We can learn new things all the time. We have expansion energy and the power within to blossom and grow.

I remember my plane trip to Israel. As we landed in Tel Aviv, I felt hesitation. I was unclear what this country or experience would hold for me. It was the year of the 60th celebration of independence and Americans were urged to take caution during international travel.

I simply wasn't the type to sit on the beach or in the hotel room. Given I had remarried at this point in my life, my current husband ventured off for business meetings; I mustered the courage to walk miles on a boardwalk to Jaffa, the oldest port city in the world. I put in my mind that fear couldn't hold me back. Along the way, I stopped at a roadside café and ate lunch. Here I wrote in my journal. I documented my feelings of stepping over fears that have held me back in life and opening myself up to new horizons.

Soon, I was standing in front of the Wishing Bridge in Jaffa. On the Wishing Bridge, I placed my hands on my zodiac sign, Aquarius, and sent my wishes out to sea. Legend says that the wish will be carried forward and I believed it. In those moments, I held two wishes-one for my sister to have a healthy birth with the twins and another for God to use me as an instrument to heal.

Upon my return, I felt a shift inside; like a newly formed conviction, that anything in life was possible. I realized that defining moments of my life were the moments where I thought much bigger than where I stood at that point in time. By acknowledging to myself that life is self-perception and harnessing our personal power, I came across women whose real stories inspired me to think bigger.

Inspiration Icons – Empowers Us

Michele Jones Galvin is a direct descendant of Harriet Tubman and co author with her mom, Joyce of *Beyond the Underground. Aunt Harriet, Moses of Her People*[23]. Michele shared with me that Aunt Harriet epitomized hope. Michele and her mother, Joyce Stokes Jones, have spent over twenty years researching historical facts and family accounts. They took a trip to Ghana,

---

[23] Sankofa Media, 2013

Africa to see the slave trade so they could properly document the journey to America.

"What makes the book different is that it's written by a relative," shares Michele. During our discussion, it was evident that the big dream to see the family story in print and share Aunt Harriet's legacy with the world was becoming a reality. Bringing this story to life has meant tenacity and a belief that bigger dreams can become realities.

Our personal power is ours to claim. It's the part of us that beckons to be awakened. It is the authentic part of ourselves that wants us to be true by honoring our values, beliefs and innately who are in this lifetime. We can choose to be joy, we can release our fears, we can believe in faith, and we can pursue the paths of our dreams, one step - one day at a time.

Periods of uncertainty will arise, when our children grow up and leave the nest, when we say goodbye to loved ones, when life hands us different circumstances than we thought we should have – but then in that space in time, we should know that rebirth can be beautiful.

I learned from my journey with Michele, the power of "dreaming a dream" and taking the steps to make a dream possible. I witnessed determination despite all obstacles, to press ahead and believe with conviction. That support champions, someone alongside of us, cheering us to the finish line, can make a huge difference.

It's in the recognition that we in our human state will be given tests of faith; life experiences and moments where we should make lemonade out of the lemons handed to us. Yet, if we recognize the small simple blessings in our life- and accept that we are special and extraordinary in our own unique ways, we will find joy in each day.

As I have traveled to different parts of the world, shared cups of tea with multicultural women, I see the beauty in our common wisdom- that we bear more in common than our differences. Community can provide enlightenment to us because we hear and listen to other people's stories. We then understand that each of us has a path to walk, and how we view the landscape of our path is entirely up to us.

As a young girl, I learned from my Nana. She shared her wisdom with other women about being in the first group of women, to have radiation in Rochester, New York, that she had an experience to share. Years later, I watched my mom as she waited in a hospital room diagnosed with breast cancer before her surgery, and saw firsthand the power of prayer. In both instances, community, faith and family support engulfed these women.

Nana and Mom became inspiration for me. Think in your own life, of those that empower you. Maybe in our daily life, it is as simple as an inspiring quote on our refrigerator, or a teacher that told us we could do it, versus one who told us that we could not. When we share our thoughts with a friend, co-worker, parent, we share an intimate moment of our self, the gift of our time.

As you come to the end of this book, recognize that all the tools to succeed are already inside of you. Your ability to *Live the Life of Your Dreams* starts with the power of intention - to do just that! Believe in tenacity;

rise up to the occasion that within you is a great strength. Know with conviction that you were created for a purpose, to serve others and carve out time to nourish the most important one, yourself.

Reader Reflections

A place for you to pen your thoughts and ideas or pause enough to notice your magnificence.

Food for Thought......

♥We learn about rebirth, and the spirit of conviction in this chapter. Reflect for a moment on your inner strength. Give yourself permission to recognize your own personal power. What areas in your life do you want to shift your energy toward or redirect your behaviors?

"We delight in the beauty of a butterfly, but rarely admit the changes it has gone through to achieve its beauty."
- Maya Angelou.

Reflections – Moving Forward

By sharing precious moments, we can grow and learn from each other's life wisdom. The butterfly image reminds us that we are constantly growing and evolving. That we like the butterfly – evolve, change and blossom.

Now that you've finished reading, what comes next? Remind yourself that *Live the Life of Your Dreams, 33 Tips for Inspired Living* is a guidebook to help you in your daily living. The power of choice resides in you to construct your daily life. Seize the opportunity to gain awareness about yourself and expand your horizons.

My hope for you is a happy tomorrow. Let go of anything that no longer serves you well. Surround yourself with images that inspire and support you. Be open to new possibilities. Be the artist to paint your own landscape. Take time just for you- nourish your mind, body and spirit. And pause long enough to notice that which surrounds you.

Carve out time each day for just you. Align your energy in motion with things or activities that sustain, or energize you. Reclaim your inner power to live the best life possible. Recognize that all roads that you walked have provided growth. Each and every moment is necessary for our soul's evolution.

Step over fear. Try new activities, and expand your willingness to grow. Just do it.

Show compassion with yourself. Be present in the grace of each day, instead of worrying about yesterday and tomorrow. And if all else fails, be still for a few minutes and hear yourself breathing. I love the quote, "On a quiet day, she could hear herself breathing."

Together, we have the brilliance to light up the sky and paint the world with hope! Our collective stories told by each of us have the power to transform our communities, each other and the greater consciousness. Share your journey with another along the road of life.

What did you learn from this experience?

- ♥ An opportunity to rediscover yourself.
- ♥ Don't let fear hold you back in life.
- ♥ To take care of yourself.
- ♥ To carve out sacred spaces and moments and be free to explore *you*.
- ♥ Dream Big Dreams. Believe in your ability to create your ideal life.

I would love to hear your inspired story. With grace and honor for your journey. *- Laura Ponticello*

Tips for Inspired Living

The number thirty-three is thought of as a sacred number in numerology and also known as a number that symbolizes guidance,[24] which is why I have 33 Daily Tips to inspire you. I believe there is great power in creating a life you desire. The days of being all things to all people are gone. While responsibilities may consume your life, self-care is critical to the nourishment of our minds, bodies and spirits.

The intentions to fill up your inner well and to sit in spaces of "quietude" to hear your inner wisdom are critical to creativity, health, and spiritual wellness. Break free of self-imposed limitations; instead redirect yourself toward creating the *Life of Your Dreams*. I encourage you to incorporate some of the inspired ideas into your daily life.

---

[24]

www.sacredscribesangelnumbers.blogspot.com/2011/06/angel-number-33.html

33 Inspired Ideas for Daily Life

- ♥ 1. Bloom where you are planted.

- ♥ 2. Concentrate on your breath.

- ♥ 3. Seek refuge in nature.

- ♥ 4. Surrender your worries.

- ♥ 5. Pursue something with passion.

- ♥ 6. Write in bite-sized bits.

- ♥ 7. Keep a gratitude journal.

- ♥ 8. Collect images to visualize your dreams.

- ♥ 9. Surround yourself with empowering words.

- ♥ 10. Release any past hurts. Forgive.

- ♥ 11. Mirror on the Wall (reinforces our psyche.)

♥ 12. Find catalysts for empowerment.

♥ 13. Visualize your dream.

♥ 14. Create sacred spaces.

♥ 15. Meditate.

♥ 16. Sit with a prayer.

♥ 17. Perform a ritual.

♥ 18. Be present in the moment.

♥ 19. Surround yourself with living things.

♥ 20. Start your day with one thing that makes you happy.

♥ 21. Everything in moderation- balanced living.

♥ 22. Add movements to your routine.

- 23. Engage in relaxation activities.

- 24. Focus on your breath.

- 25. Walk with purpose.

- 26. Make healthy choices about what you eat.

- 27. Gathering circles inspire us.

- 28. Gratitude is attitude.

- 29. Perform random acts of kindness.

- 30. Surround yourself with happiness reminders.

- 31. Create a blessings list.

- 32. Discover support champions.

- 33. Create harmonious living spaces.

About the Author

Laura Ponticello is an author, motivational speaker, thought leader and professional coach for writers, entrepreneurs and business leaders. She is the founder of Laura's List: Books for Women, an online community devoted to building connections through the power of a story. In this role, she has inspired thousands of readers and sponsored philanthropic events that raise money for important causes, such as breast cancer. Laura is also the founder of Divine Phoenix, dedicated to sharing transformational stories on a global basis.

Laura graduated Magna Cum Laude with Bachelor's degrees in Anthropology and Sociology from Canisius College in 1991. She has been recognized by Six Sigma, and has been featured in national publications.

Share the Power of Stories & Connect

♥ **If inspired, help us share universal stories of hope and inspiration.** Bring Laura to your hometown, share this book with another, donate a copy to your local library or church, post your book review on social network sites and help join the movement to empower each other.

Connect
Email: laurasbooklist@aol.com

Website: www.divinephoenixbooks.com & lauraponticello.com (speaker's page)

Facebook: LaurasList:Books for Women
Twitter: @lauraslist
Linked In: Laura Ponticello

A portion of the sales from this book will be donated to Positively Pink Packages, a 501(c)3 nonprofit, in honor of Laura's grandmother and mother, www.positivelypinkpackages.org

Made in the USA
Charleston, SC
11 May 2014